So you really want to learn

Latin
Prep

Workbook 1B

A.M. Wright

GALORE PARK

www.galorepark.co.uk

Published by Galore Park Publishing Ltd
Carmelite House, 50 Victoria Embankment, London EC4Y 0DZ
www.galorepark.co.uk

Text copyright © Anne Wright 2006
Illustrations copyright Galore Park 2006

The right of Anne Wright to be identified as the author of this Work has been asserted by her in accordance with sections 77 and 78 of the Copyright, Designs and Patents Act 1988.

Typography by Qué, Kent
Cover illustration by Ian Douglass

Printed and bound by Ashford Colour Press Ltd, Gosport, Hampshire

ISBN: 978 1 905735 14 3

First published 2006, reprinted 2007, 2008, 2010, 2011, 2013, 2014, 2015, 2016

Details of other Galore Park publications are available at www.galorepark.co.uk

ISEB Revision Guides, publications and examination papers may also be obtained from Galore Park.

Introduction

The exercises in this book will help you to practise and improve your grasp of Latin. Each exercise has been designed to reinforce what you have learned in the second half of Latin Prep 1 (Galore Park, 2006) (and therefore begins at Chapter 6) and focuses on **vocabulary**, **grammar** or **translation** work. Latin Prep Workbook 1A (ISBN-13: 9781902984674) reinforces the work covered in the first half of Latin Prep 1. Your teacher may want you to do some or all of the exercises, but each one is suitable for practice or revision. References to the new edition of Latin Prep 1 by Theo Zinn are shown by 'LP1', e.g. LP1 p.2 means page 2 of Latin Prep 1.

There is a strong focus on **grammar**, not just because over a quarter of the marks at Common Entrance are specifically based on grammar, but because you cannot produce accurate translations (at **any** level) unless you know what the words are doing and why.

How to use this book

If you are told to learn something, do so – thoroughly!

Vocabulary

✔ Learn the vocabulary for each chapter **before** you begin. When learning, try to think of English derivations (words which come from the Latin word). This will help you to remember what Latin words mean.

✔ Use vocabulary **flashcards** (Latin on one side, English on the other). This will help you to check your knowledge and focus on troublesome words. You can buy these from Galore Park (ISBN: 978 0 90362 765 8).

✔ Always remember to learn what **type** of word you are studying (noun, verb, conjunction, etc.).

✔ Always learn the **grammatical information** given (e.g., if you have to learn that **casa** means **house**, learn all the information given: **casa, -ae, f. = house**). This way you can work out all the other endings and will know what sort of words to use with it.

Grammar

✔ Always **learn** grammar thoroughly.

✔ Try to **practise** new grammar by explaining it to someone else (little brothers or sisters make good guinea pigs!). If you can explain grammar well, then you have learned it properly.

✔ **Recite** endings to yourself at regular intervals to keep them fresh (try reciting them in the shower or on the way to school).

Translation

✔ **Never guess!** Use the word endings to work out the meaning. The sooner you train yourself to concentrate on endings, the quicker you will be able to translate Latin well.

Marks

✔ The maximum number of marks available is shown at the side of the exercise. There is also a space for your score. Try to improve on your best score!

On page 46 you will find a sheet to record your scores for all the chapters.

CHAPTER 6
GRAMMAR WORK: 2nd conjugation

> **LEARNING POINT 6a**
> ✔ **Learn** the 2nd conjugation present, imperfect and perfect tenses, **LPI p.64**

These exercises use the 2nd conjugation verbs listed, LPI p.65.

Exercise 6.1 Present tense

Translate the following:

1.	terret	_____	**(I)**	( )
2.	monetis	_____	**(I)**	( )
3.	habes	_____	**(I)**	( )
4.	manemus	_____	**(I)**	( )
5.	respondeo	_____	**(I)**	( )
6.	we reply	_____	**(I)**	( )
7.	he moves	_____	**(I)**	( )
8.	you (s.) order	_____	**(I)**	( )
9.	you (pl.) frighten	_____	**(I)**	( )
10.	they advise	_____	**(I)**	( )
		TOTAL	**(10)**	( )

Exercise 6.2

Change the verb to the plural and translate the new form:

1.	moveo	_____	**(2)**	( )
2.	times	_____	**(2)**	( )
3.	delet	_____	**(2)**	( )
4.	manes	_____	**(2)**	( )
5.	iubeo	_____	**(2)**	( )
		TOTAL	**(10)**	( )

Exercise 6.3

Change the verb to the singular and translate the new form:

1. tenemus _____

   _____ (2) ( )

2. deletis _____

   _____ (2) ( )

3. timent _____

   _____ (2) ( )

4. monemus _____

   _____ (2) ( )

5. manent _____

   _____ (2) ( )

                                              TOTAL (10) ( )

Exercise 6.4   Imperfect tense

Translate the following:

1. delebant _____ (1) ( )
2. ridebas _____ (1) ( )
3. monebamus _____ (1) ( )
4. iubebam _____ (1) ( )
5. videbat _____ (1) ( )
6. you (s.) were destroying _____ (1) ( )
7. they were fearing _____ (1) ( )
8. we were remaining _____ (1) ( )
9. I was laughing _____ (1) ( )
10. he was frightening _____ (1) ( )

                                              TOTAL (10) ( )

Exercise 6.5

Change the verb to the plural and translate the new form:

1. timebam _____

    _____ **(2)** ( )

2. movebas _____

    _____ **(2)** ( )

3. tenebat _____

    _____ **(2)** ( )

4. delebas _____

    _____ **(2)** ( )

5. respondebam _____

    _____ **(2)** ( )

                                                   TOTAL (10) ( )

Exercise 6.6

Change the verb to the singular and translate the new form:

1. delebamus _____

    _____ **(2)** ( )

2. habebatis _____

    _____ **(2)** ( )

3. movebant _____

    _____ **(2)** ( )

4. respondebatis _____

    _____ **(2)** ( )

5. monebamus _____

    _____ **(2)** ( )

                                                   TOTAL (10) ( )

Exercise 6.7 Perfect tense

Translate the following:

1. vidisti _____ **(1)** ( )
2. monuistis _____ **(1)** ( )
3. terruit _____ **(1)** ( )
4. iusserunt _____ **(1)** ( )
5. respondi _____ **(1)** ( )

6.	he has destroyed	(1)	( )
7.	we have seen	(1)	( )
8.	you (pl.) have moved	(1)	( )
9.	I have feared	(1)	( )
10.	you (s.) have warned	(1)	( )
		TOTAL (10)	( )

Exercise 6.8

Change the verb to the plural and translate the new form:

1. mansi _____ (2) ( )

2. habuisti _____ (2) ( )

3. terruit _____ (2) ( )

4. delevi _____ (2) ( )

5. risit _____ (2) ( )

TOTAL (10) ( )

Exercise 6.9

Change the verb to the singular and translate the new form:

1. movimus _____ (2) ( )

2. delevistis _____ (2) ( )

3. tenuerunt _____ (2) ( )

4. respondistis _____ (2) ( )

5. monuimus _____ (2) ( )

TOTAL (10) ( )

Exercise 6.10

Translate these sentences. Note that present, imperfect and perfect tenses are used.

1. olim nautae muros oppidorum deleverunt.

    _____

    _____ **(5)** ( )

2. 'cur ad insulam navigatis?' magister clamavit. 'undas magnas timemus,' servi

    responderunt. _____

    _____ **(10)** ( )

3. turba magna in oppido diu manebat.

    _____

    _____ **(6)** ( )

4. servos in agrum vocavimus. non festinaverunt.

    _____

    _____ **(6)** ( )

5. magistri pueros malos monebant. pueri tamen non laborabant.

    _____

    _____ **(8)** ( )

6. The slaves were moving the food.

    _____

    _____ **(4)** ( )

7. I warned the girl. She did not reply.

    _____

    _____ **(5)** ( )

8. We used to laugh in the big fields.

    _____

    _____ **(5)** ( )

9. The bad inhabitants destroy the walls of the town.

    _____

    _____ **(6)** ( )

10.   We feared the farmers and the teachers.

_____

_____ **(5)**   ( )

                                        TOTAL **(60)**   ( )

GRAMMAR WORK: apposition, pronouns and questions

LEARNING POINT 6b
✔ **Learn** the information about apposition, **LP1 p.68**
✔ **Learn** the information about pronouns, **LP1 p.68**
✔ **Learn** the information about questions, **LP1 p.70**

Exercise 6.11

Translate the following sentences:

1.   ubi nautae navigaverunt? quinque ad nos navigabant sed tres ad insulas

navigaverunt. _____

_____ **(11)**   ( )

2.   cur Decimus, filius magistri, librum non portat?

_____

_____ **(7)**   ( )

3.   viri oppidum oppugnaverunt; turba incolarum muros oppidi delevit.

_____

_____

_____ **(8)**   ( )

4.   equus malus me terruit sed Iulius, amicus puellarum pulchrarum, equum

non timebat. _____

_____

_____ **(11)**   ( )

5.   nos trans undas navigabamus et iam oppidum oppugnamus.

_____

_____ **(8)**   ( )

6.   Did she sail to the islands?

_____

_____ **(4)**   ( )

7.   **I** was fighting, but **you** (s.) overcame me.

_____

_____ **(7)**   ( )

8.   For a long time we used to fear the teacher.

_____

_____ **(4)**   ( )

9.   Why did you (pl.) kill the man?

_____

_____ **(4)**   ( )

10.   The crowd killed the man with many arrows.

_____

_____ **(6)**   ( )

TOTAL **(70)**   ( )

GRAMMAR WORK: the 3rd conjugation

LEARNING POINT 6c
    ✔ **Learn** the 3rd conjugation present, imperfect and perfect tenses, **LP1 p.73**

All exercises use the 3rd conjugation verbs listed on **LP1 p.73**
Exercise 6.12
State the tense of each verb and translate:

1.   discedebamus   _____

_____ **(2)**   ( )

2.   duxit   _____

_____ **(2)**   ( )

3.   luditis   _____

_____ **(2)**   ( )

4.   ostendebant   _____

_____ **(2)**   ( )

5. scripsistis _____

_____ **(2)** ( )

6. you (pl.) depart _____

_____ **(2)** ( )

7. they were leading _____

_____ **(2)** ( )

8. you (s.) wrote _____

_____ **(2)** ( )

9. she leads _____

_____ **(2)** ( )

10. I have read _____

_____ **(2)** ( )

TOTAL **(20)** ( )

Exercise 6.13

State the tense of each verb, change the verb to the plural and translate the new form.

1. dicebam _____

_____ **(3)** ( )

2. legis _____

_____ **(3)** ( )

3. ducit _____

_____ **(3)** ( )

4. lusi _____

_____ **(3)** ( )

5. legebas _____

_____ **(3)** ( )

TOTAL **(15)** ( )

Exercise 6.14

State the tense of each verb, change the verb to the singular and translate the new form.

1. rexerunt _____

_____ **(3)** ( )

2. scribebatis _____

_____ **(3)** ( )

3. discesserunt _____

    _____ **(3)** ( )

4. ostenditis _____

    _____ **(3)** ( )

5. ludebant _____

    _____ **(3)** ( )

                                    TOTAL (15) ( )

Exercise 6.15

Translate these sentences. Note that present, imperfect and perfect tenses are used.

1. in libris puerorum magister verba multa scripsit.

    _____

    _____ **(7)** ( )

2. agricola de patria dixit et de periculo monuit.

    _____

    _____ **(7)** ( )

3. vir Spurio, amico bono, multa dicebat.

    _____

    _____ **(6)** ( )

4. 'quid dixisti?' agricola rogabat. 'ubi est aqua? estne in vino?' dixi.

    _____

    _____

    _____ **(11)** ( )

5. vir malus incolas hastis terruit et incolas diu regebat.

    _____

    _____

    _____ **(9)** ( )

6. You (pl.) used to rule the town.

    _____

    _____ **(3)** ( )

7. The happy girls played with the horses.

    _____

    _____ **(6)** ( )

8. Have you read the book? I have read the books.

    _____

    _____ **(6)** ( )

9. Why did you (pl.) lead the slaves to the island?

    _____

    _____ **(6)** ( )

10. I showed the spears to the woman.

    _____

    _____ **(4)** ( )

                                           TOTAL (65) ( )

CONSOLIDATION

Exercise 6.16 Comprehension

Read the following passage and then answer the questions on it:

> **Despite the help of Aeolus, Ulysses (Odysseus) is unable to return home**
>
> olim Ulixes et nautae a patria **Troianorum** discesserunt et ad Graeciam festinabant; sed, **propter** iram deorum, trans undas altas diu navigabant. in magno periculo erant. tandem Ulixes insulam **vidit**. 'nautae,' clamavit, 'hic est insula.'

Troianus, -i, m. = Trojan
propter + acc. = because of, on account of
video, videre, vidi, visum = I see

1. Who was sailing? (line 1)

    _____ **(2)** ( )

2. What route were they taking? (lines 1-2)

    _____ **(2)** ( )

3. Quote and translate the Latin word in line 3 that shows the time spent sailing.

    _____ **(2)** ( )

4. We are told that the men were in great danger (line 3). Explain what was the specific danger and why it had occurred.

    _____

    _____ **(2+2)** ( )

5.   What did Ulixes see and when? (lines 3-4)

_____

_____ **(2)** ( )

6.   How did he react to this? (line 4)

_____

_____ **(3)** ( )

TOTAL (15) ( )

Exercise 6.17 Translation

Translate the following passage:

1	viri fessi in insulam festinaverunt et tandem incolam **viderunt**. 'quis es?' Ulixes rogavit. 'Aeolus, dominus ventorum, sum,' incola viris dixit. Aeolus ventos rexit. ventos multos in **sacco posuit** et nautis **saccum** dedit. unus ventus in **sacco** non erat. tandem Ulixes et nautae ad patriam navigaverunt sed nautae **saccum aperuerunt**.
5	

video, videre, visi,
visum = I see
saccus, -i, m. = sack, bag
pono, ponere, posui,
positum = I put, I place
aperio, aperire, aperui,
apertum = I open

_____

_____

_____

_____

_____

_____

_____

_____

_____

_____

_____

_____

_____

_____

_____

TOTAL (30) ( )

Exercise 6.18 Grammar

Read the following passage and then answer the questions on it:

venti e **sacco** festinaverunt. miser Ulixes clamavit, 'cur, nautae, **saccum aperuistis**? iam venti nos a patria **pellunt**. di nos superaverunt; ad patriam non **redibimus**.'	**saccus, -i, m.** = sack, bag **aperio, aperire, aperui, apertum** = I open **pello, pellere, pepuli, pulsum** = I drive **redibimus** = we shall return

1. From the passage, give an example of:

    (a) a preposition used with an accusative noun _____ **(1)** ( )

    (b) an adverb _____ **(1)** ( )

2. In which case is each of the following nouns and why?

    venti (line 1) _____ **(2)** ( )

    nautae (line 2) _____ **(2)** ( )

3. State the tense and person of **clamavit** (line 1) and give the 1st person singular present tense form.

    _____

    _____ **(3)** ( )

4. State the Latin subject and object of **pellunt** (line 3).

    Subject _____ Object _____ **(2)** ( )

5. In line 3, we are told that 'the gods have overcome us' (di nos superaverunt). What change would you need to make to **superaverunt** if you wanted to say 'the gods **were** overcoming us'?

    _____

    _____ **(1)** ( )

6. Give an English word derived from **miser** (line 1) and explain the connection between the Latin and English words.

    _____

    _____

    _____

    _____ **(3)** ( )

7.   Translate into Latin: The farmers were warning the beautiful girls.

_____

_____

_____ **(5)**   ( )

                                            TOTAL (20)   ( )

                        CONSOLIDATION TOTAL (65)   ( )

CHAPTER SIX	MAXIMUM SCORE	400/400	=	100%
	MY SCORE	/400	=	%

GRAMMAR

CHAPTER 7
GRAMMAR WORK: numerals

> **LEARNING POINT 7a**
> ✔ **Learn** the information about ordinals, **LP1 p.76**
> ✔ **Revise** the information about cardinal numbers, **LP1 p.52**

Exercise 7.1

Translate the following:

1. quartus puer cum quinta puella ambulabat.

   _____
   _____ **(6)** ( )

2. ubi est secundus equus, serve?

   _____
   _____ **(5)** ( )

3. feminae ad septimum dominum cibum portant.

   _____
   _____ **(6)** ( )

4. prope agros eramus et in tertio muro stetimus.

   _____
   _____ **(8)** ( )

5. decimus vir sextum servum necabat sed tertiam ancillam magnopere laudavit.

   _____
   _____
   _____ **(10)** ( )

6. Why did the sixth boy fight?

   _____
   _____ **(5)** ( )

7. We hurried with the fourth friend.

   _____
   _____ **(5)** ( )

8.   The three poets sang the first word.

_____

_____ **(6)**   ( )

9.   The ninth sailor sails across the high waves.

_____

_____ **(7)**   ( )

10. The teacher of the girls enters into the second field.

_____

_____ **(7)**   ( )

TOTAL (65)   ( )

GRAMMAR WORK: 4th conjugation

> **LEARNING POINT 7b**
> ✔ **Read** and **learn** the information on 4th conjugation verbs, **LP1 p.77**

Exercise 7.2
State the tense of each verb and then translate:

1.   dormiverunt   _____

_____ **(2)**   ( )

2.   veniebat   _____

_____ **(2)**   ( )

3.   dormis   _____

_____ **(2)**   ( )

4.   audiebamus   _____

_____ **(2)**   ( )

5.   audivisti   _____

_____ **(2)**   ( )

6.   you (pl.) slept   _____

_____ **(2)**   ( )

7.   they hear   _____

_____ **(2)**   ( )

8.   we sleep _____

_____ **(2)**   ( )

9.   she came _____

_____ **(2)**   ( )

10. they were hearing _____

_____ **(2)**   ( )

TOTAL **(20)**   ( )

Exercise 7.3

State the tense of each verb, change the verb to the plural and translate the new form:

1.   audiebas _____

_____ **(3)**   ( )

2.   dormit _____

_____ **(3)**   ( )

3.   veni _____

_____ **(3)**   ( )

4.   veniebat _____

_____ **(3)**   ( )

5.   audivisti _____

_____ **(3)**   ( )

TOTAL **(15)**   ( )

Exercise 7.4

State the tense of each verb, change the verb to the singular and translate the new form:

1.   venitis _____

_____ **(3)**   ( )

2.   venistis _____

_____ **(3)**   ( )

3.   dormiebatis _____

_____ **(3)**   ( )

4.   audivimus _____

_____ **(3)**   ( )

5.   dormiunt _____

_____ **(3)   ( )**

TOTAL (15)   ( )

Exercise 7.5

Translate these sentences. Note that present, imperfect and perfect tenses are used.

1.   'cur, Marce, dormiebas et non laborabas?' magister iratus rogavit.

_____

_____

_____ **(9)   ( )**

2.   tres servi ex oppido venerunt. equos dominorum duxerunt.

_____

_____

_____ **(8)   ( )**

3.   mox verba magistri audivimus et in agros festinavimus.

_____

_____

_____ **(8)   ( )**

4.   puellae in agris stabant sed pueros non audiebant.

_____

_____

_____ **(7)   ( )**

5.   'cur ad templum festinas?' 'quod poetae multi veniunt!'

_____

_____

_____ **(8)   ( )**

6.   The happy boys were sleeping in the fields.

_____

_____

_____ **(6)   ( )**

7. The friend of the maid-servant does not come.

_____

_____

_____ **(5)**   ( )

8. We heard the men because they were shouting.

_____

_____

_____ **(5)**   ( )

9. 'Why are you (s.) sleeping?' the teacher was asking.

_____

_____

_____ **(5)**   ( )

10. You (s.) heard the goddess again.

_____

_____

_____ **(4)**   ( )

TOTAL **(65)**   ( )

GRAMMAR WORK: infinitive

LEARNING POINT 7c

✔ The **infinitive** is the **2nd principal part** and means **'to' do something**.

e.g. amo, **amare**, amavi, amatum   amare = to love

There are different forms of the infinitive according to the conjugation:

1st	amo, amare	3rd	rego, regere
2nd	moneo, monere	4th	audio, audire

Exercise 7.6

Translate the following:

Note: constituo, constituere, constitui, constitutum = I decide

1. dominus servum laborare iussit.

_____

_____ **(4)**   ( )

2. nautas ad insulam navigare iubemus.

   _____

   _____ **(5)** ( )

3. regina patriam regere tandem constituit.

   _____

   _____ **(5)** ( )

4. turba virorum bella timuit sed pugnare constituit

   _____

   _____

   _____ **(7)** ( )

5. auxilio deorum oppidum oppugnare constituistis; agricolae et incolae igitur festinant.

   _____

   _____

   _____

   _____ **(9)** ( )

6. I decide to hurry through the fields.

   _____

   _____ **(5)** ( )

7. He decides to praise the daughter.

   _____

   _____ **(4)** ( )

8. At last we decided to enter the temple.

   _____

   _____ **(5)** ( )

9. I love to hear the words of the poets.

   _____

   _____ **(5)** ( )

10. I do not see the son. He loves to fight.

    _____

    _____ **(6)** ( )

    TOTAL (55) ( )

CONSOLIDATION

Exercise 7.7 Comprehension

Read the following passage and then answer the questions on it:

> **A wise queen is given some bad advice**
> olim dearum poeta bonus reginam monuit, 'agricolae Romani secundum oppidum hastis et sagittis oppugnaverunt. itaque hic stare et muros aedificare **debemus**.' reginae ira magna erat sed poetam non audivit. novem viris tamen dixit, 'viri, a muris oppidi ambulare **debetis**.'

> debeo, debere, debui
> = I must, I ought

1. Who warned the queen? (line 1) _____
   _____ **(2)** ( )

2. Who was armed and how? (lines 1-2) _____
   _____ **(3)** ( )

3. Why did this cause concern? (lines 1-2) _____
   _____ **(2)** ( )

4. What advice was offered? _____
   _____ **(4)** ( )

5. How did the queen feel in line 3? _____
   _____ **(1)** ( )

6. In line 4, what did the queen tell the men to do? _____
   _____ **(3)** ( )

   TOTAL **(15)** ( )

Exercise 7.8 Translation

Translate the following passage:

> 1 unus vir, 'cur?' rogavit. regina respondit, 'nautas trans undas altas et prope oppidum ducere **debetis**.' regina viros de periculo magno monuit. tandem viri ex oppido venerunt. mox Romani oppidum iterum oppugnabant sed viri, quod nautas duxerunt, Romanos superaverunt. diu et fortiter pugnabant;
> 5 Romanos multos igitur viri necaverunt.

> debeo, debere, debui
> = I must, I ought

_____

_____

_____

_____
_____
_____
_____
_____
_____
_____
_____
_____
_____
_____
_____

TOTAL (30)   ( )

Exercise 7.9 Grammar

Read the following passage and then answer the questions on it:

iam patria <u>tuta</u> et regina laeta erat. regina itaque viris pecuniam dedit. viri fessi in oppidum festinaverunt et, quod regina poetam non audivit, reginam pulchram laudaverunt.	tutus, -a, -um = safe

1.   Give an example of:

    (a) a 1st declension masculine noun _____ **(1)   ( )**

    (b) a verb in the imperfect tense_____ **(1)   ( )**

2.   In which case are the following nouns and why?

    viris (line 1) _____

    _____ **(2)   ( )**

    oppidum (line 2) _____

    _____ **(2)   ( )**

3.   State the Latin subject and object of **audivit** (line 2):

    Subject _____ Object _____ **(2)   ( )**

4.   State the tense and person of **laudaverunt** (line 3) and give the 1st person

    singular present tense form. _____

    _____ **(3)   ( )**

5. In lines 1-2, we are told that 'the tired men hurried' (viri fessi festinaverunt). What change would you need to make to **fessi** if you wanted to say 'the tired **women** hurried'?

    _____ **(1)** ( )

6. In line 1, we are told that 'the queen gave money' (regina pecuniam dedit). What change would you need to make to **dedit** if you wanted to say 'the queen **gives** money'?

    _____ **(1)** ( )

7. What does **audivit** mean? Explain the connection between audivit and the English word **audition**.

    _____

    _____

    _____ **(3)** ( )

8. Translate into Latin: We were fighting in the war.

    _____ **(4)** ( )

    TOTAL **(20)** ( )

    CONSOLIDATION TOTAL **(65)** ( )

CHAPTER SEVEN	MAXIMUM SCORE	300/300	=	100%
	MY SCORE	/300	=	%

CHAPTER 8
GRAMMAR WORK: the mixed conjugation

LEARNING POINT 8a
✔ **Read** and **learn** the information on mixed conjugation verbs, **LP1 pp.85-86**

Exercise 8.1

State the tense of each verb and then translate:

1. cupiebat _____

    _____ **(2)** ( )

2. fecistis _____

    _____ **(2)** ( )

3. cepi _____

    _____ **(2)** ( )

4. iaciebamus _____

    _____ **(2)** ( )

5. cupiunt _____

    _____ **(2)** ( )

6. we were making _____

    _____ **(2)** ( )

7. they take _____

    _____ **(2)** ( )

8. you (pl.) threw _____

    _____ **(2)** ( )

9. they were wishing _____

    _____ **(2)** ( )

10. she throws _____

    _____ **(2)** ( )

                                            TOTAL (20) ( )

Exercise 8.2

State the tense of each verb, change the verb to the plural and translate the new form:

1. cupiebas _____

    _____ (3)   ( )

2. capio _____

    _____ (3)   ( )

3. fecit _____

    _____ (3)   ( )

4. iacit _____

    _____ (3)   ( )

5. capiebam _____

    _____ (3)   ( )

    TOTAL **(15)**   ( )

Exercise 8.3

State the tense of each verb, change the verb to the singular and translate the new form:

1. cupiebamus _____

    _____ (3)   ( )

2. ceperunt _____

    _____ (3)   ( )

3. iacitis _____

    _____ (3)   ( )

4. cupiunt _____

    _____ (3)   ( )

5. iaciebatis _____

    _____ (3)   ( )

    TOTAL **(15)**   ( )

Exercise 8.4

Translate these sentences. Note that present, imperfect and perfect tenses are used.

1. nuntius gladium cepit et in proelium festinavit.

   _____

   _____ **(6)** ( )

2. socii hastas et sagittas saepe iaciebant.

   _____

   _____ **(6)** ( )

3. vir clarus scuta nova semper fecit.

   _____

   _____ **(6)** ( )

4. cur puellam notam audire non cupitis?

   _____

   _____ **(6)** ( )

5. a deo saevo statim navigare cupiebamus.

   _____

   _____ **(6)** ( )

6. You (s.) were making wine.

   _____

   _____ **(3)** ( )

7. The allies capture the messenger.

   _____

   _____ **(4)** ( )

8. The poet wished to sing.

   _____

   _____ **(4)** ( )

9. We threw the gold into the sky.

   _____

   _____ **(5)** ( )

10. They captured the terrified farmer.

    _____

    _____ **(4)** ( )

    TOTAL (50) ( )

GRAMMAR

GRAMMAR WORK: the imperative

LEARNING POINT 8b
- ✔ **Learn** the information about imperatives, **LP1 pp.88-89**
- ✔ **Learn** the information about irregular imperatives, **LP1 p.89**

Exercise 8.5

Highlight the imperative in each sentence and translate:

1. domine, filios specta!

    _____

    _____ **(3)**   ( )

2. ab oppido currite!

    _____

    _____ **(3)**   ( )

3. serve, in agrum intra et equos duc!

    _____

    _____ **(4)**   ( )

4. servos feminarum iube in agris laborare!

    _____

    _____ **(6)**   ( )

5. aquam amico statim da!

    _____

    _____ **(4)**   ( )

6. Prepare the food, girls!

    _____

    _____ **(4)**   ( )

7. Sleep immediately, boys!

    _____

    _____ **(4)**   ( )

8. Maid-servant, warn the queen!

    _____

    _____ **(4)**   ( )

9.   Take the horse, daughter!

_____

_____ **(4)**   ( )

10.   Take the horses, daughters!

_____

_____ **(4)**   ( )

TOTAL **(40)**   ( )

GRAMMAR WORK: compounds of sum

LEARNING POINT 8c
✔ **Learn** the information about compounds of sum, **LP1 pp. 92-93**
✔ **Remember**: the infinitive of sum is esse
✔ **Note:** The imperatives of sum are es and este

Exercise 8.6
Translate the following:

1.   in proelio incolae multi adfuerunt.

_____

_____ **(5)**   ( )

2.   multi nautae a patria aberant.

_____

_____ **(5)**   ( )

3.   afuisti; servi igitur non laborabant.

_____

_____ **(4)**   ( )

4.   'boni este,' magister pueris clamabat.

_____

_____ **(5)**   ( )

5.   pueri tamen, 'mali esse cupimus,' dixerunt.

_____

_____ **(6)**   ( )

6.   They have been absent for a long time.

   _____

   _____   **(3)**   ( )

7.   The friend of the queen is present.

   _____

   _____   **(4)**   ( )

8.   We were away from the town.

   _____

   _____   **(4)**   ( )

9.   You (pl.) were wanting to be present in the field.

   _____

   _____   **(5)**   ( )

10.   The teacher was not present.

   _____

   _____   **(4)**   ( )

                                                    TOTAL (45)   ( )

CONSOLIDATION

LEARNING POINT 8d
   ✔ **Revise** the use of prepositions, **LP1 p.41 and p.53**

Exercise 8.7 Comprehension

Read the following passage and then answer the questions on it:

> **A queen sends help to her allies**
> nuntius sociorum ad oppidum festinavit. reginae notae dixit 'socii in periculo
> magno sunt. nautae validi agros et templa saepe oppugnant.' reginae ira
> magna erat. viros vocavit; mox aderant. regina turbae virorum dixit 'statim
> scuta et gladios capite et ad patriam sociorum festinate. nautas necate!'

1.   Who was hurrying? (line 1)

   _____   **(2)**   ( )

2.   To whom did he speak in lines 1-2?

   _____   **(2)**   ( )

3.   What did he say that the sailors were doing? (line 2)

_____

_____ **(4)**   ( )

4.   How would you describe the queen's mood? (lines 2-3)

_____

_____ **(1)**   ( )

5.   Whom did she call in line 3? How quickly did they come?

_____

_____ **(2)**   ( )

6.   The queen gave many orders – translate two of them.

_____

_____

_____ **(4)**   ( )

TOTAL **(15)**   ( )

Exercise 8.8 Translation

Translate the following passage:

> itaque viri cum nuntio in patriam mox venerunt. nautas diu spectaverunt.
> tandem agricola, **qui** viros ducebat, 'in undas festinate!' iussit. in undis contra
> nautas fortiter pugnaverunt. mox nautae magnopere timebant et multi a
> proelio saevo trans undas altas navigaverunt.

qui = who

_____

_____

_____

_____

_____

_____

_____

TOTAL **(30)**   ( )

Exercise 8.9 Grammar

Read the following passage and then answer the questions on it:

> tandem nautae afuerunt. incolae **non iam** perterriti erant sed in oppido
> laeti aderant. aurum nautarum ceperunt et templum novum dis
> aedificaverunt. viri clari ad patriam **revenerunt**. regina clamavit, 'dic,
> agricola, de bello.' agricola de proelio saevo dixit et deos laudavit.

non iam = no longer
**revenio, revenire,
reveni** = I return

1. From the passage give an example of:

   (a) a noun in the genitive _____ **(1)** ( )

   (b) an imperative _____ **(1)** ( )

2. In which case is **bello** (line 4) and why?

   _____

   _____ **(2)** ( )

3. In line 3, we are told that 'the queen shouted' (**regina clamavit**). What
   change would you need to make to **clamavit** if you wanted to say 'the queen
   was shouting'?

   _____ **(1)** ( )

4. What does **dixit** (line 4) mean? Explain the connection between dixit and the
   English word **contradict**.

   _____

   _____

   _____ **(3)** ( )

5. State the tense of **afuerunt** (line 1) and give the 1st person singular present
   tense form.

   _____

   _____ **(2)** ( )

6. In lines 2-3, we are told that 'they built a new temple' (**templum novum
   aedificaverunt**). What change would you need to make to **templum** if you
   wanted to say 'they built new **temples**'?

   _____

   _____ **(1)** ( )

7. Translate into Latin: The teachers wish to walk.

   _____

   _____ **(4)** ( )

8.   Translate into Latin: The terrified farmers were carrying shields.

_____

_____ (5)   ( )

TOTAL (20)   ( )

CONSOLIDATION TOTAL (65)   ( )

CHAPTER EIGHT	MAXIMUM SCORE	250/250	=	100%
	MY SCORE	/250	=	%

CHAPTER 9
GRAMMAR WORK: subordinate clauses

> **LEARNING POINT 9a**
> ✔ **Read** and **learn** the information on subordinate clauses, **LP1 p.97**

Exercise 9.1

Underline the main clause in green and the subordinate clause in blue.
Then translate. Remember that **ubi** can mean **when** as well as **where**.

1. incolae, ubi regina oppidum subito delevit, perterriti erant.

    _____

    _____

    _____ **(8)** ( )

2. nuntius tuus, ubi in templum intravit, deas Romanas magnopere laudavit.

    _____

    _____

    _____ **(10)** ( )

3. ancillae, quod nauta hastas et sagittas portabat, ex agris discedere cupiebant.

    _____

    _____

    _____ **(11)** ( )

4. verba poetae, quod pulchra erant, scribere constitui.

    _____

    _____

    _____ **(7)** ( )

5. pueri, ubi in agris currebant, equos dominorum saepe spectabant.

    _____

    _____

    _____ **(9)** ( )

6. We built the walls because we feared the allies.

    _____

    _____

    _____ **(6)** ( )

7.   The sailors, when they sailed to the island, were tired.

_____

_____ **(8)** ( )

8.   We sent help to the inhabitants because they are our friends.

_____

_____ **(8)** ( )

9.   The boys, because they are happy, want to run into the waves.

_____

_____

_____ **(9)** ( )

10.   When there was danger to the fatherland, you (pl.) were wanting many swords.

_____

_____

_____ **(9)** ( )

TOTAL **(85)** ( )

LEARNING POINT 9b
✔ **Revise** verb endings (including infinitives and imperatives) and vocabulary

Exercise 9.2

State the tense of each verb and translate:

1.   veniunt   _____

_____ **(2)** ( )

2.   eramus   _____

_____ **(2)** ( )

3.   discesserunt   _____

_____ **(2)** ( )

4.   oppugnate   _____

_____ **(2)** ( )

5.   dedit   _____

_____ **(2)** ( )

6.	we were attacking	_____	
		_____	**(2)** ( )
7.	I sailed	_____	
		_____	**(2)** ( )
8.	you (pl.) were hearing	_____	
		_____	**(2)** ( )
9.	you (s.) had been absent	_____	
		_____	**(2)** ( )
10.	to make	_____	
		_____	**(2)** ( )
		TOTAL	**(20)** ( )

LEARNING POINT 9c

✔ **Revise** noun case endings, the meanings of cases and vocabulary

Exercise 9.3

State the case and translate:

1.	a proelio	_____	
		_____	**(2)** ( )
2.	filiarum	_____	
		_____	**(2)** ( )
3.	feminas	_____	
		_____	**(2)** ( )
4.	serve	_____	
		_____	**(2)** ( )
5.	prope templa	_____	
		_____	**(2)** ( )
6.	with swords	_____	
		_____	**(2)** ( )
7.	O, girls!	_____	
		_____	**(2)** ( )

8.   for the inhabitant _____
     _____ **(2)** ( )

9.   wars (obj.)   _____
     _____ **(2)** ( )

10. of the man   _____
     _____ **(2)** ( )
                                      TOTAL (20) ( )

LEARNING POINT 9d
✔ **Revise** adjective endings and vocabulary

Exercise 9.4

State the number, case and gender and translate:

1.   filiorum sacrorum _____
     _____
     _____ **(3)** ( )

2.   incolas fessos   _____
     _____
     _____ **(3)** ( )

3.   ad proelia saeva   _____
     _____
     _____ **(3)** ( )

4.   o femina valida   _____
     _____
     _____ **(3)** ( )

5.   cum puellis bonis _____
     _____
     _____ **(3)** ( )

6.   a tall wall (obj.) _____
     _____
     _____ **(3)** ( )

7.   O bad farmers!

_____

_____

_____ **(3)**   ( )

8.   with the big arrow

_____

_____

_____ **(3)**   ( )

9.   of the small sailors

_____

_____

_____ **(3)**   ( )

10.   beautiful towns (subj.)

_____

_____

_____ **(3)**   ( )

TOTAL **(30)**   ( )

GRAMMAR WORK: adverbs

LEARNING POINT 9e
✔ **Learn** the information about adverbs, **LP1 p.103**

Exercise 9.5
Highlight the adverb. Write in a bracket whether it is of place, time or manner and then translate the sentence.

1.   turba virorum oppida nostra subito oppugnavit.

_____

_____

_____ **(2+6)**   ( )

2.   gladiis in proelio saevo fortiter pugnabamus.

_____

_____

_____ **(2+6)**   ( )

3. libros statim portare servos fessos iussi.

   _____

   _____

   _____ **(2+6)** ( )

4. ibi in caelo sunt di magni.

   _____

   _____ **(2+6)** ( )

5. amici socius de bello bene dixit.

   _____

   _____ **(2+6)** ( )

6. Where are the bad daughters of the teacher?

   _____

   _____

   _____ **(2+8)** ( )

7. We often used to build walls.

   _____

   _____ **(2+5)** ( )

8. 'Wait!' I shouted, 'you (s.) greatly fear the farmers.'

   _____

   _____ **(2+6)** ( )

9. Soon we were seeing the small waves.

   _____

   _____ **(2+5)** ( )

10. Once you (pl.) decided to give horses to the woman.

    _____

    _____ **(2+6)** ( )

    TOTAL (80) ( )

CONSOLIDATION

Exercise 9.6 Comprehension

Read the following passage and then answer the questions on it:

> **_I am told about a terrible threat_**
> ubi nuntius intravit ego cum amicis vinum et aquam bibebam.
> 'audite me,' clamavit; 'est magnum periculum: **monstrum**
> saevum! in undis habitabat sed ex undis discessit et in **terram**
> venit. puellas necavit! festinate et monstrum necate!'

monstrum, -i, n. = monster
terra, -ae, f. = land

1. What was the narrator doing at the beginning of the story? (line 1)

    _____ **(3)** ( )

2. Who interrupted them in lines 1-2?

    _____ **(1)** ( )

3. What did he say was causing great danger? (lines 2-3)

    _____

    _____ **(2)** ( )

4. (Lines 3-4) Why was this a new threat? Give details

    _____

    _____

    _____ **(4)** ( )

5. What dreadful thing had it done? (line 4) _____

    _____ **(2)** ( )

6. What did the man want them to do about this matter? (line 4) _____

    _____ **(3)** ( )

    TOTAL (15) ( )

Exercise 9.7 Translation

Translate the following passage:

| 1 | virum audivimus sed non discessimus. deinde Iulius clamavit, 'contra **monstrum** pugno!' agricola 'gladium, Iuli, cape!' dixit et Iulio gladium dedit. ad undas currebat et cum Iulio trans agros et prope undas etiam ambulabamus. ibi stetimus sed Iulius ad **monstrum** venit. '**monstrum**,' |
| 5 | clamavit, 'auxilio deorum et gladio agricolae te neco!' |

monstrum, -i, n.
= monster

_____

_____

_____

_____

_____

_____

_____

_____

_____

_____

_____

_____

_____

TOTAL (30) ( )

Exercise 9.8 Grammar

Read the following passage and then answer the questions on it:

monstrum non cucurrit. dormiebatne? deinde Iulius 'monstrum, te pugnare iubeo!' monuit et in monstrum gladium iecit. iterum monstrum non cucurrit itaque 'monstrum superavi!' vocavit. sed monstrum **balaena mortua** erat. sic Iulius monstrum delevit!

monstrum, -i, n. = monster

mortuus, -a, -um = dead
balaena, -ae, f. = whale

1. From the passage give an example of:

(a) a noun in the vocative _____ **(1)** ( )

(b) a 1st person singular perfect verb _____ **(1)** ( )

2. In which case is **gladium** and why (line 2)?

_____

_____ **(2)** ( )

3. State the tense and person of **iecit** (line 2) and give the 1st person singular,

present tense form. _____

_____

_____ **(3)** ( )

4. What is the 3rd principal part of **iubeo** (line 2)? _____ **(1)** ( )

5. What is the purpose of −ne (line 1)? _____

_____ **(1)** ( )

6. In lines 1-2, we are told that 'Julius warned' (Iulius monuit). What change
   would you need to make to **monuit** if you wanted to say 'Julius **warns**'?

_____ **(1)** ( )

7. What does **gladium** mean? Explain the connection between gladium and the
   English word **gladiator**.

_____

_____

_____

_____ **(3)** ( )

8. Translate into Latin: You (s.) used to have many maid-servants.

_____

_____ **(4)** ( )

9. Translate into Latin: We attacked the towns.

_____

_____ **(3)** ( )

TOTAL **(20)** ( )

CONSOLIDATION TOTAL **(65)** ( )

CHAPTER NINE	MAXIMUM SCORE	300/300	=	100%
	MY SCORE	/300	=	%

CHAPTER 10
CONSOLIDATION

Exercise 10.1 Comprehension

Read the following passage and then answer the questions on it:

> **Aeneas escapes from Troy**
>
> 1   decimos annos Graeci Troiam oppugnabant. Graeci tandem oppidum
> Troiam ceperunt et deleverunt. viros miseros et feminas perterritas in
> viis et etiam in templis necaverunt. Aeneas, ubi Graecos vidit, discedere
> paravit. cum amicis suis in undas navigavit. in loco tuto oppidum novum
> 5   **condere** cupivit.

condo, condere,
condidi, conditum
= I found, build

1.   In lines 1-2, what had happened to Troy?

                                             (3) ( )

2.   When had this happened?

                                             (1) ( )

3.   Name one group who were killed. (lines 2-3)

                                             (2) ( )

4.   In which places were they killed? (lines 2-3)

                                             (2) ( )

5.   How did Aeneas react? (lines 3-4)

                                             (2) ( )

6.   With whom did he sail? (line 4)

                                             (1) ( )

7.   What did he want to do? (lines 4-5)

                                             (4) ( )

                                         TOTAL (15) ( )

Exercise 10.2 Translation

Translate the following passage:

> ### Mercury reminds Aeneas of his duty after he meets Dido
>
> 1 tandem ad terram pulchram venerunt. amici subito viros audiverunt. turba
> magna incolarum muros et templa aedificabat. deinde vir reginae **Aenean** et
> socios ostendit. regina 'manete' dixit 'et cibum consumite!' amici itaque
> manere constituerunt. Dido **Aenean** magnopere amabat sed Mercurius,
> 5 nuntius deorum, viro dixit, 'cur hic manes? ad patriam novam statim naviga!'

Aenean:
acc. s. of
Aeneas

TOTAL (30) ( )

Exercise 10.3 Grammar

Read the following passage and then answer the questions on it:

Aeneas leaves to seek a new Troy in Italy

1 Aeneas nuntio non respondit sed ad socios cucurrit et de nuntio
  nuntiavit; deinde trans undas navigaverunt. Dido Aenean non videbat;
  igitur timebat. 'numquam adest. Aeneasne me non amat?' deinde
  ancilla vinum prope reginam posuit. Dido vinum bibit, gladium cepit
5 et tenuit. caelum spectabat et dixit 'di **immortales**, me spectate.
  mortem mihi mittite!'

immortales = immortal
mortem = death
mihi = to me

---

1. Give examples from the passage of:

   an imperative _____

   a dative noun _____ **(2)** ( )

2. In which case is **undas** and why (line 2)?

   _____

   _____ **(2)** ( )

3. In line 1, we are told that Aeneas ran (Aeneas cucurrit). What change would
   you need to make to **cucurrit** if you wanted to say 'Aeneas **runs**'?

   _____ **(1)** ( )

4. Translate **timebat** (line 3) and suggest an English derivation. Explain the
   connection between the two words.

   _____

   _____

   _____ **(3)** ( )

5. State the person, tense and 1st person singular, present tense form of **cepit**
   (line 4).

   _____

   _____ **(3)** ( )

6. State the subject and object of **tenuit** (line 5).

   Subject _____ Object _____ **(2)** ( )

7. Translate into Latin: The happy sailors laugh.

   _____ **(4)** ( )

8. Translate into Latin: The masters were singing.

_____ (3)   ( )

TOTAL (20)   ( )

CHAPTER TEN	MAXIMUM SCORE	65/65	=	100%
	MY SCORE	/65	=	%

SCORES

HOW DID YOU DO?

Keep a record of your scores as you work through the book. By the time you reach Chapter 10, you should be scoring 70% or above. If you're not, go back, revise the material, and try again! Practice makes perfect.

	My score	Max score	My %
Chapter 6	_____	400	_____
Chapter 7	_____	300	_____
Chapter 8	_____	250	_____
Chapter 9	_____	300	_____
Chapter 10	_____	65	_____